GARDEN FLOWERS
IN SUGAR

T O N Y   W A R R E N

M E R E H U R S T

This book is dedicated to my family: my daughter Emily, my son Matthew, my wife Alma, and my three sisters, Barbara, Gladys and Pam, for all their help and support.

First published in 1996 by Merehurst Limited, Ferry House, 51 – 57 Lacy Road, Putney, London SW15 1PR
Copyright © Merehurst Limited 1996
ISBN 1 85391 567 X

Edited by Alison Leach
Designed by Jo Tapper
Photography by James Duncan
Colour separation by Pixel Tech. Pte Ltd, Singapore
Printed by Wing King Tong, Hong Kong

Acknowledgements
My everlasting thanks go to Tombi Peck for typing most of the script. Without her help and advice I would never have finished this book. She, along with Alan Dunn, kept me sane (or is it insane?).
Great Impressions, Greenlea, 14 Studley Drive, Swarland, Morpeth, Northumberland NE65 9JT.
Tinkertech Two (icing cutters), 40 Langdon Road, Parkstone, Poole, Dorset BH14 9EH.
Confectionery Supplies, 27 Eign Road, Hereford HR1 2RU.
Celcakes, Springfield House, Gate Helmsley, York YO4 1NF.
Orchard Products, 49 Langdale Road, Hove, East Sussex BN3 4HR.
Swifts Bakery, 5 Parkway, Ludlow, Shropshire SY8 2PG.
Florabunda Florist, 152 Corve Street, Ludlow, Shropshire SY8 2PG.
Holly Products, Holly Cottage, Hassell Green, Sandbach, Cheshire CW11 0YA. Paul Maddox for supplying the cake boards and stand. Lesley Herbert for the idea of making leaves. I would like to thank Barbara Croxford, James Duncan, Jo Tapper and Alison Leach, for all their help and guidance in this book.

The publisher would like to thank the following for their assistance:
Anniversary House (Cake Dec.) Ltd., Unit 5, Roundways, Elliott Road, Bournemouth, BH11 8JJ, Tel: 01202 590222; Cake Art Ltd., Venture Way, Crown Estate, Priorswood, Taunton, TA2 8DE, Tel: 01823 321532; Guy, Paul & Co., Ltd., Unit B4, Foundry Way, Little End Road, Eaton Socon, Cambridge PE19 3JH, Tel: 01480 472545; Squires Kitchen, 3 Waverley Lane, Farnham, Surrey, GU9 8BB, Tel: 01252 711749.

NOTES ON USING THE RECIPES
For all recipes, quantities are given in metric, Imperial and cup measurements. Follow one set of measures only as they are not interchangeable. Standard 5ml teaspoons (tsp) and 15ml tablespoons (tbsp) are used. Australian readers, whose tablespoons measure 20ml, should adjust quantities accordingly. All spoon measures are assumed to be level unless otherwise stated.
Eggs are a standard size 3 (medium) unless otherwise stated.

CONTENTS

INTRODUCTION

*W*hen I left school, I trained as a chef but I always had a special interest in cake decorating. I first heard about sugarcraft when my eldest sister Barbara started taking classes with Muffie Mackenzie. I was so fascinated by what she was learning that it did not take long before I too went to the classes with her. I was totally captivated by sugarcraft to such an extent that I decided to make it my full-time occupation.

I entered my first competition in 1990 in London's biennial Hotelympia where I won a Silver Medal for a celebration cake. This inspired me even more and so I entered again in 1992 when I was awarded a Gold Medal for a wedding cake. To my delight, I won another in the 1994 exhibition. Although I do enjoy competition work, I am always so busy demonstrating and giving lessons, as well as making and decorating cakes to order, that I do not have enough time to enter many competitions.

In this, my first, book I have chosen the kind of flowers I would like to grow in my own garden. Colour is of course always an important factor when designing cakes and the innumerable shades of garden flowers range from the strong yellow of sunflowers to the soft pink of dianthus, making very different effects possible.

Especially for wedding receptions when the cake should be a focal point, I try to make my designs quite striking and I think the Casablanca lilies on the three-tier cake add a distinctive element to the arrangement. For birthdays and other celebrations, the Terracotta Flower Container cake would be particularly suitable for any keen gardener.

I hope you enjoy strolling around my imaginary garden as much as I have enjoyed planning and writing this book.

EQUIPMENT

❖

Most sugarcraft enthusiasts will already have most of the equipment for the flowers and cakes illustrated. Templates have been provided for the cutters but the actual metal or plastic cutters do make life easier. They will save a lot of time especially if you have lots of flowers to make.

A selection of wires has been used from the thinner 30-gauge for the smaller flowers up to 18-gauge wire for the larger ones. The wires are available in white or different shades of green, but the 18-gauge wire is usually uncovered. If you do not have the appropriate colour you can always cover them with stemtex of the right shade. It is also handy to have different coloured florist tape.

A varied selection of stamens is always useful as is some very fine thread for making your own.

Veiners are available in many varieties both for petals and leaves. Most of the leaves have been given a shine with confectioner's glaze which I have used in different strengths: full glaze, three-quarter glaze which is ¾ glaze to ¼ isopropyl alcohol, half-glaze which is ½ glaze to ½ isopropyl alcohol and quarter-glaze which is ¼ glaze to ¾ isopropyl alcohol.

A selection of good quality dusting brushes is essential. Paste colourings and dusting powders (petal dusts/blossom tints) may be mixed together to achieve a larger range of colours.

ROYAL ICING FOR LACE WORK

❖

1 size 2 egg white (string removed)
250g (8 oz/1½ cups) sifted icing (confectioners') sugar

● Put the egg white in a grease-free bowl of an electric mixer and carefully add the sifted icing sugar. When all the sugar has been mixed with the egg white, turn the mixer to its lowest speed and beat the icing for 4 minutes.

● Store the icing in a clean grease-free airtight container, covering with cling film (plastic wrap) before attaching the lid.

ROYAL ICING WITH MERI-WHITE

❖

4 tsp Meri-white
90ml (3 fl oz/6 tbsp) cold water
500g (1 lb/3 cups) sifted icing (confectioners') sugar

● Dissolve the Meri-white in the cold water in a grease-free mixing bowl of an electric mixer. Gradually add the sifted icing sugar, using the lowest speed of the mixer. Beat for 4–6 minutes, until the icing forms full peaks.

● Store the icing in a grease-free airtight container, cover with cling film (plastic wrap) before attaching the lid.

Some of the more useful items of equipment are illustrated clockwise from top right: Paste colourings, craft knife, plastic cutters, dusting powders (petal dusts/blossom tints), leaf and petal veiners, tape shredder, metal cutters, impression mat, scriber, tweezers, curved scissors, palette knife, texturing tool, dog bone tool, Dresden tool, floristry tape, celpad, rolling pin, paint and dusting brushes, stamens, thread, small rolling pin, silk veining tool, confectioner's glaze and wires.

PASTILLAGE

❖

1 tsp gum tragacanth
1 quantity royal icing made with Meri-white
about 375g (12 oz/2¼ cups) sifted icing
(confectioners') sugar

◯ Stir the gum tragacanth into the royal icing and leave for 24 hours. Then add enough icing sugar to make a firm paste and knead thoroughly until smooth. Wrap in cling film (plastic wrap) and store in an airtight container.

FLOWER PASTE

❖

A heavy-duty electric mixer is used in this recipe.

5 tsp cold water
2 tsp powdered gelatine
500g (1 lb/3 cups) sifted icing (confectioners')
sugar
3 tsp gum tragacanth
2 tsp liquid glucose
4 tsp white vegetable fat (shortening)
1 size 2 egg white (string removed)

◯ Put the cold water in a heatproof bowl, sprinkle gelatine over the water and leave to stand for 30 minutes.

◯ Put the sifted icing sugar into the bowl of a heavy-duty electric mixer. Sprinkle the gum tragacanth over the surface. Place the bowl in a preheated oven 100°C (200°F/Gas ¼) for about 30 minutes to warm the sugar. Warm the liquid glucose until it is soft.

◯ Dissolve the gelatine over a pan of hot water. Remove from the heat and add the softened glucose and white vegetable fat. Stir over a low heat until dissolved.

◯ Place the bowl of warmed sugar on the mixer. Add the dissolved gelatine mixture and the egg white.

◯ Cover the mixer with a clean, dry cloth and switch on to the lowest speed. Mix until all ingredients are combined. Then turn to high speed and beat until the paste becomes white. Underbeating results in the paste remaining off-white and too soft.

◯ Remove the paste from the bowl and cover with cling film (plastic wrap). Place in an airtight container in the refrigerator. Leave to mature for 24 hours before use.

COLOURINGS USED ON CAKES AND FLOWERS

❖

Sundial Wedding Cake
(clematis and honeysuckle)
Paste Colourings: chestnut, Christmas green, claret, melon and spruce green.
Dusting Powders (Petal Dusts/Blossom Tints): aubergine, champagne, coral, cornflower blue, forest green, lemon, moss green, nutkin brown, plum, primrose, red and violet.
Pearl Lustre Colourings: apple and lilac.

Terracotta Plant Container
(geraniums, begonias, lobelia and nicotiana)
Paste Colourings: bitter lemon, black, blueberry, chestnut brown, Christmas green, cream, dark brown, gooseberry, melon, mulberry and spruce green.
Dusting Powders (Petal Dusts/Blossom Tints): burgundy, deep purple, moss green, nutkin brown, pink, plum, primrose, spring green and white.

Detail of Tea Rose

Dianthus Christening Cake
(dianthus and pram)
Paste Colourings: blueberry, melon, mulberry, ruby and spruce green.
Dusting Powders (Petal Dusts/Blossom Tints): moss green and pink.

Casablanca Fantasy Wedding Cake
(Casablanca lilies, Solomon's seal, ivy leaves and roses)
Paste Colourings: Christmas green, gooseberry, melon, mint green and spruce green.
Dusting Powders (Petal Dusts/Blossom Tints): aubergine, forest green, moss green, nutkin brown, primrose, skintone, spring green and tangerine.

Golden Wedding Cake
(tea roses, sunflowers and ivy)
Paste Colourings: Christmas green, dark brown, egg yellow and spruce green.
Dusting Powders (Petal Dusts/Blossom Tints): egg yellow, jade, lemon, moss green, nutkin brown, plum and red.

Candlestick Crescent
(philadelphus)
Paste Colouring: spruce green.
Dusting Powders (Petal Dusts/Blossom Tints): apple green, aubergine, burgundy, egg yellow, forest green, lemon, moss green, nutkin brown and plum.

Fuchsia
Paste Colourings: mulberry, navy blue, ruby and spruce green.
Dusting Powders (Petal Dusts/Blossom Tints): burgundy, moss green and nutkin brown.

Snowdrops
Paste Colourings: Christmas green and tangerine.
Dusting Powders (Petal Dusts/Blossom Tints): moss green, navy blue and white.

Peony
Paste Colourings: Christmas green, dark brown, gooseberry, mulberry and spruce green.
Dusting Powders (Petal Dusts/Blossom Tints): aubergine, moss green and plum.

Dutch Iris
Paste Colourings: Christmas green and gooseberry.
Dusting Powders (Petal Dusts/Blossom Tints): deep purple, lavender, lemon and moss green.

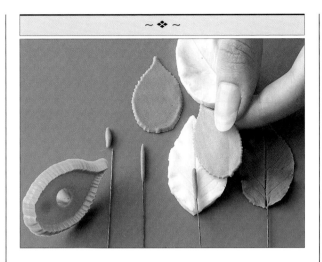

~ ❖ ~

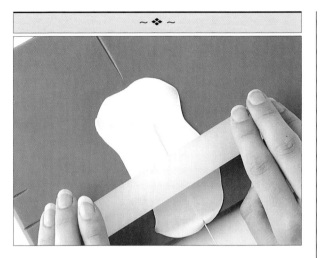

~ ❖ ~

MAKING LEAVES USING A DOUBLE-SIDED VEINER

❖

This method of making leaves will save a great deal of time.

● Roll out a piece of green flower paste and cut out leaves, using either a template or a cutter. Cover them to prevent them from drying out.

● Roll a thin sausage of flower paste onto one end of a 28-gauge wire and place the sausage in the bottom half of a double-sided veiner. Place a leaf on top, then the top half of the veiner and press together. Remove the leaf from the veiner, soften the edges and allow to dry.

INSERTING WIRES INTO LONG PETALS AND LEAVES

❖

This method allows you to bend the petals so that they hold their shape and it also strengthens them.

● Roll out a piece of flower paste over a grooved board and place a wire over the groove. The gauge of wire depends on the size of petals and leaves being used.

● Roll the wire into the paste and cut out petal or leaf shapes, using either templates or cutters. Vein the petals and soften the edges in the usual manner. If the wires are protruding out of the ends of the petals, cut off with wire cutters.

SUNDIAL WEDDING CAKE

15cm (6 in) round cake
30cm (12 in) teardrop cake
apricot glaze
2kg (4 lb) marzipan (almond paste)
clear alcohol (gin or vodka)
2.5kg (5 lb) ivory sugarpaste
Royal Icing, see page 6
selection of paste food colourings
selection of dusting powders (petal dusts/blossom tints)
pastillage, see page 8

EQUIPMENT
20cm (8 in) round cake board
38cm (15 in) teardrop cake board
greaseproof paper (parchment)
scriber
no. 1, 2 and 0 piping tubes (tips)
paintbrushes
sheet of perspex (plexiglass)
tilting display stand
non-slip matting
3.25m (3½ yd) ribbon to trim boards
piping gel

FLOWERS
7 honeysuckle stems, see page 14
5 honeysuckle buds, see page 14
66 honeysuckle leaves, see page 14
7 clematis, see page 16
35 clematis buds, see page 16
63 clematis leaves, see page 16

Detail of brush embroidery

● Brush cakes with apricot glaze and cover with marzipan. Allow to dry. Brush the cakes and boards with clear alcohol and cover with sugarpaste. Make sure the large section of the teardrop cake is to the right, so that it fits around the column of the stand. When dry, place the cakes on boards.

● Trace the brush embroidery designs onto greaseproof paper, see pages 16 and 18. Ensuring that all pencil lines are on the outside, secure the designs to the sides of the cakes with pins. Scribe each cake design, then remove the templates. Add 1 tsp piping gel to 250g (8oz) royal icing.

● Pipe the flower stems first and then the leaves with a no. 1 tube, using Christmas green royal icing for the honeysuckle and chestnut brown for the clematis.

● Pipe the clematis flowers and buds using a no. 2 tube with pale claret royal icing and pipe the leaves using a no. 1 tube with Christmas green royal icing. When dry, dust the flowers with violet and a little cornflower blue dusting powders mixed together. Dust the leaves with moss green dusting powder. Pipe the stamens using a no. 0 tube and paint them with pale melon paste food colouring. Dust the flowers with plum, red, coral and moss green dusting powders and the leaves with forest green.

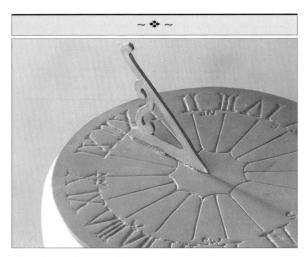

Detail of the sundial and gnomon

● Pipe an ivory royal icing border around the base of each cake using a no. 2 tube. Trim the boards with ribbon.

● To make the sundial, trace the template on page 69. Using a no. 1 tube, pipe the design in royal icing directly onto a sheet of perspex. Leave to dry. Colour a piece of sugarpaste with chestnut paste food colouring and roll out about 3mm (⅛ in) thick. Cut out a 15cm (6 in) round plaque. Press the royal icing side of the perspex sheet into the sugarpaste, lift off the sheet and leave to dry. Dust with lilac and apple pearl lustre colourings. (These colourings are not edible so the sundial must be removed before cutting the cake.)

EXPERT ADVICE

≈

As honeysuckle and clematis are climbing plants, they will look more natural if you intertwine the stems when wiring them.

● Roll out a piece of chestnut pastillage 2mm (¹⁄₁₆ in) thick and cut out the gnomon, using the template on page 69. Leave to dry, then dust as the dial.

● Secure the dial to the round cake with dots of royal icing and then secure the gnomon in the position shown in the photograph on the left.

● To assemble the cakes, position the teardrop cake on the stand first, then place the round cake on a piece of non-slip matting and position on the stand, as shown in the photograph. Arrange the flowers in place on the stand.

HONEYSUCKLE
❖

● Begin by rolling a piece of pale melon paste into a Mexican hat with a long stem. Cut out shape with honeysuckle cutter or use templates on page 19. Place flower on celpad. Soften edges with ball tool. Using a celstick, gently draw back the long petal and cup the four smaller ones. Turn flower over and open the throat using celstick. Then follow the step-by-step instructions opposite.

● Dust leaves with forest green and nutkin brown dusting powders and glaze with half-strength glaze.

● Wire leaves together in pairs alternately with 6 or 10 leaves to a stem in various sizes. When wiring, add 18- and 20-gauge wires for strength as the stems are long and need support.

~ 1 ~

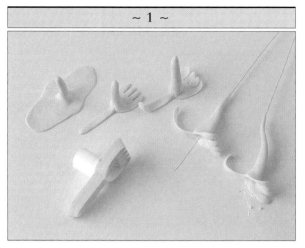

Moisten tip of a 30-gauge white wire and thread down throat of flower. Roll stem down wire so that it is slender-looking and bend stem into shape. Gently curve 5 white miniature silk stamens and a pistil and insert in throat of flower.

~ 2 ~

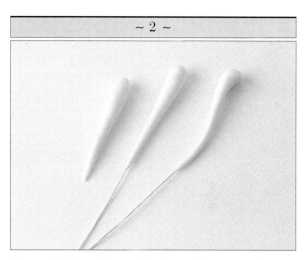

***Buds** Roll a piece of pale melon paste into a long teardrop shape. Moisten tip of a 30-gauge white wire, thread up stem and bend into shape (the buds vary in size).*

~ 3 ~

Using a 20-gauge wire, wire buds, starting with smallest ones and finally adding open flowers. When wired, dust with champagne, lemon, red, coral, aubergine and plum dusting powders. Use moss green for base.

~ 4 ~

***Leaves** Roll out spruce green paste and cut out leaves in various sizes (see templates on page 19). Moisten tip of a 28-gauge green wire and press into paste. Vein and soften edges with ball tool. Leave to dry.*

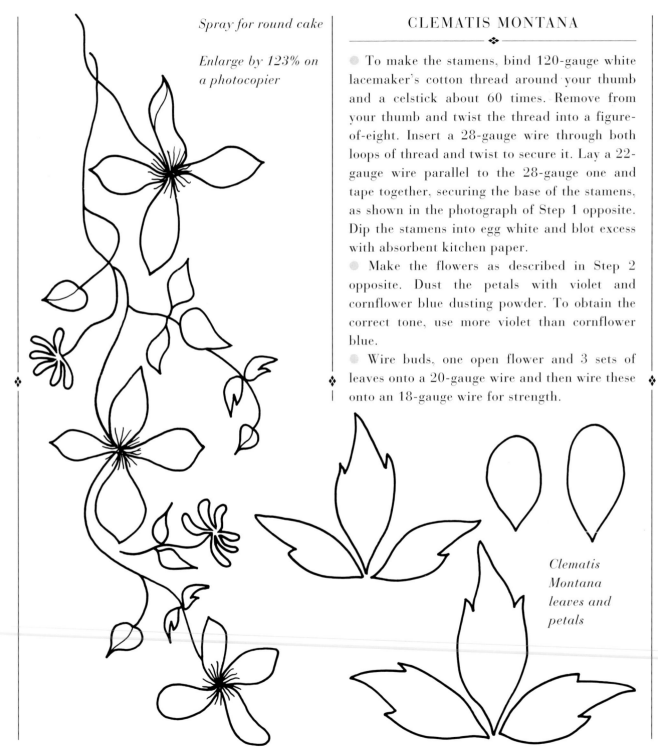

Spray for round cake

Enlarge by 123% on a photocopier

CLEMATIS MONTANA

❖

To make the stamens, bind 120-gauge white lacemaker's cotton thread around your thumb and a celstick about 60 times. Remove from your thumb and twist the thread into a figure-of-eight. Insert a 28-gauge wire through both loops of thread and twist to secure it. Lay a 22-gauge wire parallel to the 28-gauge one and tape together, securing the base of the stamens, as shown in the photograph of Step 1 opposite. Dip the stamens into egg white and blot excess with absorbent kitchen paper.

Make the flowers as described in Step 2 opposite. Dust the petals with violet and cornflower blue dusting powder. To obtain the correct tone, use more violet than cornflower blue.

Wire buds, one open flower and 3 sets of leaves onto a 20-gauge wire and then wire these onto an 18-gauge wire for strength.

Clematis Montana leaves and petals

~ 1 ~

STAMENS *Cut top of the stamens with scissors and separate them out, leaving the longer ones in centre and cutting the outer ones shorter. Dust longer stamens with moss green and outer ones with pale primrose dusting powder.*

~ 2 ~

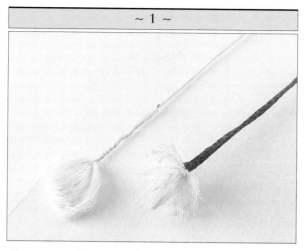

FLOWER *Roll out pale claret paste on a grooved board and cut out 4 petals. Roll a 30-gauge white wire into each petal and soften edges with ball tool. Vein with clematis veiner and leave to dry in the appropriate position.*

~ 3 ~

LEAVES *Roll out green paste on a grooved board. Cut out 3 leaves, the middle leaf being larger. Press wire into leaves and vein with clematis veiner. Soften edges with ball tool. Dust with moss green and aubergine dusting powders. Glaze with half-strength glaze.*

~ 4 ~

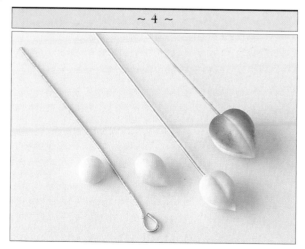

BUDS *Roll a ball of cream paste to a slight point and cut twice into paste with scissors, leaving 4 marks in paste. Make buds in various sizes. Dust with moss green and aubergine dusting powders.*

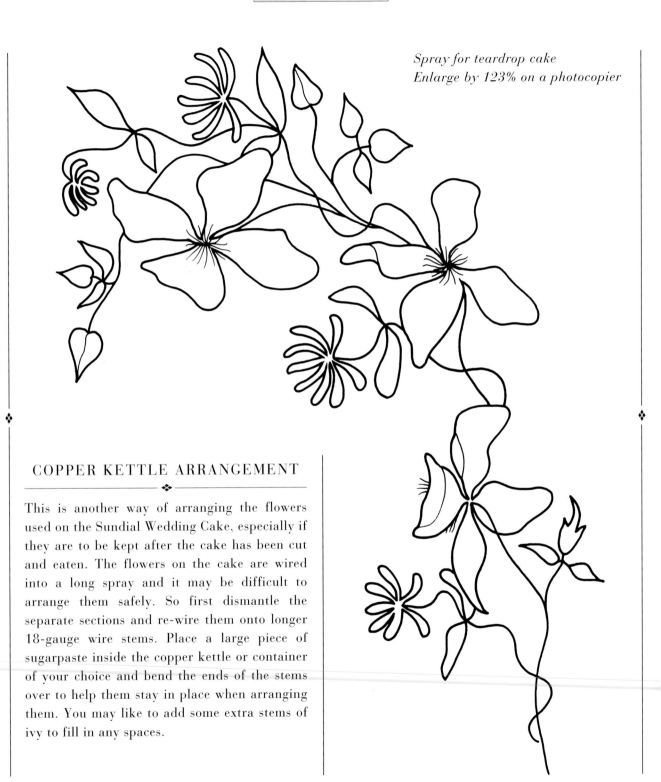

Spray for teardrop cake
Enlarge by 123% on a photocopier

COPPER KETTLE ARRANGEMENT

❖

This is another way of arranging the flowers used on the Sundial Wedding Cake, especially if they are to be kept after the cake has been cut and eaten. The flowers on the cake are wired into a long spray and it may be difficult to arrange them safely. So first dismantle the separate sections and re-wire them onto longer 18-gauge wire stems. Place a large piece of sugarpaste inside the copper kettle or container of your choice and bend the ends of the stems over to help them stay in place when arranging them. You may like to add some extra stems of ivy to fill in any spaces.

Honeysuckle petals   *Honeysuckle leaves*

TERRACOTTA PLANT CONTAINER

18cm (7 in) hexagonal cake
23cm (9 in) hexagonal cake
apricot glaze
1.25kg (2½ lb) marzipan (almond paste)
clear alcohol (gin or vodka)
375g (12 oz) grey sugarpaste
1.75g (3½ lb) chestnut sugarpaste
cornflour (cornstarch)
250g (8 oz) dark brown sugarpaste
EQUIPMENT
greaseproof paper (parchment)
30cm (12 in) hexagonal cake board
brick embossing mat
plastic acorn edging mould
claygun
1.25m (1⅓ yd) grey ribbon to trim board
FLOWERS
2 open begonias, see page 22
1 begonia bud, see page 22
16 leaves, various sizes, see page 24
13 open geraniums, see page 26
16 geranium buds, see page 26
25 leaves, various sizes, see page 26
11 open nicotiana flowers, see page 28
13 nicotiana buds, see page 29
36 nicotiana leaves, see page 29
25 open lobelia, see page 30
30 lobelia buds, see page 30
as many tiny leaves as required, see page 30

Place the larger hexagonal cake on grease-proof paper, brush with apricot glaze and place the smaller cake immediately on top of the larger one. Cut the sides to the shape shown by the dotted lines in the diagram on this page. Brush the cake with apricot glaze and cover

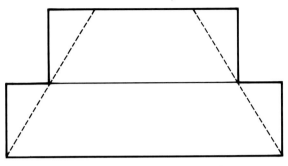

Cut cakes as shown by dotted lines

with marzipan. Allow to dry.

Brush the board with clear alcohol and cover with the grey sugarpaste. Place the brick embossing mat on the coated board and press down with a cake smoother, moving the mat until the entire board is evenly marked. Allow the board to dry.

Brush the cake with clear alcohol, cover with chestnut sugarpaste and allow to dry. Turn the cake over onto the board. Brush the top of the cake with apricot glaze and cover with marzipan. Allow to dry. Brush the cake with clear alcohol and cover with the dark brown sugarpaste. Allow to dry.

Mix a little water with some chestnut sugar-paste to make a glue which will be used to attach the moulding to the sides of the coated cake.

Roll a piece of chestnut sugarpaste into a sausage the length of the acorn edging mould. Dust the sugarpaste with cornflour and press firmly into the mould. Trim the sugarpaste level with the top of the mould and carefully remove by inverting onto a surface lightly dusted with cornflour. Turn the moulded paste over and brush the cut surface with the sugarpaste glue. Carefully pick up the sugarpaste and stick to the top edge of the cake to form a rim around the dark coated surface. Repeat this process for

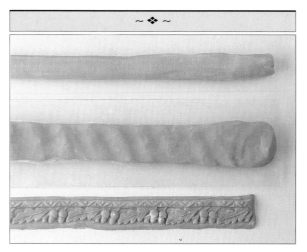

~ ❖ ~

Detail of the terracotta pot edging

the base of the cake, bevelling the edging to the embossed board.

⬤ To decorate the corners of the container, place some chestnut sugarpaste in a claygun, fitted with a rope disc. It may be necessary to add a little white vegetable fat (shortening) to the sugarpaste to soften it sufficiently to extrude easily from the claygun. Press out lengths of paste, twisting each one into a rope design. Fasten these ropes vertically to the angles of the container sides, using the sugarpaste glue.

⬤ To decorate the upper surface of the cake, press some dark brown sugarpaste through a kitchen sieve (strainer) and put onto a baking sheet to dry. Then crumble gently to create a soil effect. Moisten the dark sugarpaste surface and sprinkle with the crumbled sugarpaste.

⬤ Arrange the flowers in the container, allowing the lobelia to trail gracefully over the edge. The nicotiana adds height to the arrangement and should be placed towards the back.

BEGONIA

❖

⬤ To make a bud, hook a 22-gauge wire and moisten the hook. Make a small cone of white flower paste and insert the hook into the broad base. Flatten the cone slightly and cover the wire with green floristry tape. Roll out a piece of white flower paste and cut out 2 petals using a single rose petal cutter. Frill the edge of one petal slightly with a Dresden tool. Place on a celpad and cup the centre. Soften the edge of the second petal on a celpad with a dogbone tool and cup gently. Join the petals as described in Step 1 opposite.

⬤ Dust the bottom of the bud with spring green dusting powder.

⬤ Roll out another piece of white flower paste and cut out 2 very small rose petal shapes. Soften the edges, vein down the centre of each shape with the veining tool and attach below the bud, pointed end up, to form a pair of bracts. One bract fits over the other. Dust with a little spring green dusting powder.

⬤ To make a flower, roll a small ball of white flower paste into a cone shape. Hook a 22-gauge wire and moisten. Roll out a piece of white flower paste and using a small 5-petalled

EXPERT ADVICE

≈

When making leaves prepare a range of glazes in quarter, half, three-quarter and full strengths. This is done by mixing confectioners' glaze in wide-necked jars using different proportions of glaze and isopropyl alcohol. Measure the proportions carefully; otherwise the leaves could all look uniform.

~ 1 ~

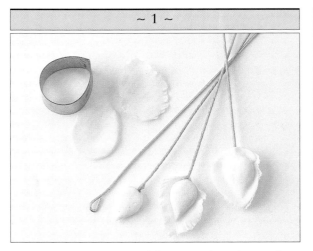

BUD *Moisten centre of first petal and attach to cone, leaving frilled edge exposed around cone. Moisten centre of second petal and attach to cone, fastening edge of petal to frilled petal tightly, being careful not to flatten frilled edge.*

~ 2 ~

FLOWER *Pull the wire with the cone through centre of blossom shape and wrap the 3 moistened petals around cone in a spiral, interlocking them. Fold the 2 remaining petals in half and attach to cone as shown. Dust base of petals with a little spring green dusting powder.*

~ 3 ~

Roll out white flower paste and using a large sweet pea standard cutter, cut out 2 petals. Elongate to a slight point and soften edges. Vein using a ceramic veining tool. Turn petals over, cupping back of each one. Attach to back of flower, opposite one another. Allow to dry.

~ 4 ~

LEAF *Soften edge lightly with a dogbone tool and vein with a begonia leaf reiner. Place on ungrooved side of board and using a Dresden tool, pull out small sections of paste to form serrations around edge of leaf. Allow to dry until firm but not hard.*

blossom cutter, or trace the template opposite, cut out 2 shapes. Keeping one of the blossom shapes covered to prevent it from drying out, place the other shape on a celpad and elongate each petal to form a point. Soften the edges, and vein using a ceramic veining tool. Using a Dresden tool, make an accentuated vein down the centre of each petal and cup with a ball tool. Moisten 2 adjoining petals and one opposite them. Follow the instructions in Step 2 on page 23.

Place the second blossom shape on the celpad, working each petal as before. Dust the centre of the shape with a little spring green dusting powder. Thread this shape onto the wire, slightly moistening the centre. Moisten the 2 petals which match the 2 folded petals, tucking them inside the folded petals on the cone. Moisten the remaining 3 petals and arrange around the cone. Dust the bottom of the flower with a little spring green dusting powder.

To make the third and fourth layers of the flower, roll out a piece of white flower paste and cut out 2 blossom shapes, using a slightly larger blossom cutter. Cover one blossom shape to prevent it drying out. Place the other shape on a celpad, and work as before, turning the shape over before cupping the petals. Thread the wire through the centre and arrange around the previous layer. It is advisable to hang the flower upside down at this stage, allowing the petals to become firm before adding the fourth layer in the same way. Allow to dry.

Roll out another piece of white flower paste and cut out 2 more blossom shapes, using a slightly larger cutter. These fifth and sixth layers are worked as for the third and fourth layers, dusting with spring green dusting powder between layers. To complete the flower,

follow the instructions in Step 3 on page 23. The template opposite for the back petal may be used instead of a cutter.

If the larger outer petals begin to fall away from the inner ones, hang the flower to dry. Dust with a little spring green dusting powder. Dust the outer edges of the flowers with pale pink petal dusting powder.

To make a leaf, colour a quantity of flower paste mid green using Christmas green and spruce green paste colourings. Roll out a piece of green paste on a grooved board, then roll a 24-gauge wire into the paste in the groove, making sure it is well embedded. Lift the wired piece of paste carefully so the wire does not bend and turn it over so that the ridge is on top. Cut out a leaf shape and place on a celpad. Follow the instructions in Step 4 on page 23.

Dust the leaf with moss green dusting powder adjusting the colour with apple green and nutkin brown to give an interesting variation on the leaf. Accentuate the edge of the leaf with burgundy dusting powder. Allow to dry. Glaze the leaf with three-quarter strength confectioners' glaze.

WIRING THE PLANT TOGETHER

Start with a large flower with a group of leaves wired in below it. Bend stems of leaves at 90° angles. Arrange buds peeping out between lower leaves into a natural-looking plant shape. Tape ends of wires, ensuring that they will fit into a posy pick for insertion into the cake.

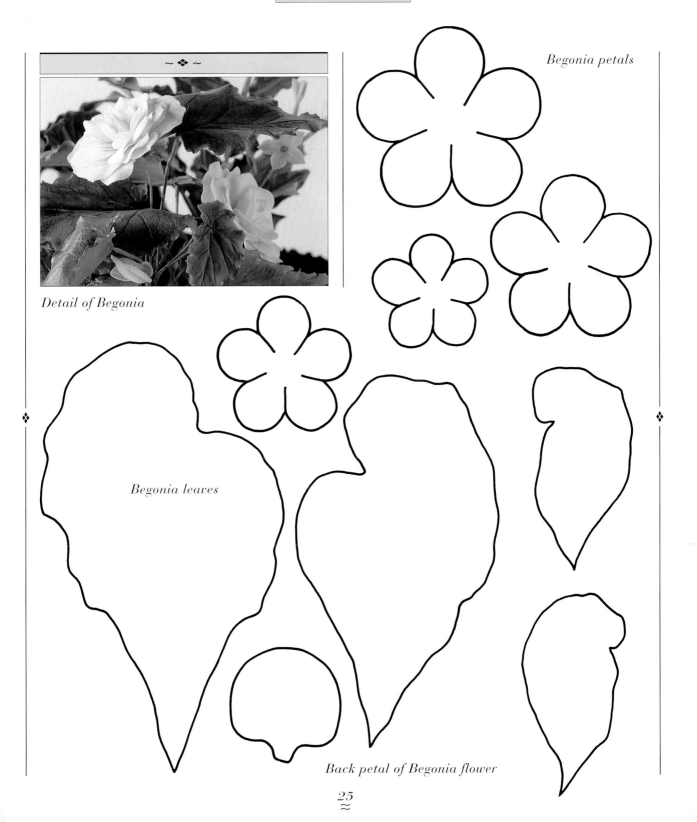

~ ❖ ~

Begonia petals

Detail of Begonia

Begonia leaves

Back petal of Begonia flower

GERANIUM

❖

To make the flowers, first tape 6 white stamens and one coarse red stamen to a 26-gauge wire. Remove the tip from the red stamen and undo it slightly so that the white shows through. Roll out a piece of mulberry coloured flower paste into a small Mexican hat and follow the instructions in Steps 1 and 2 opposite. It may be necessary to hang the geranium upside down on a stand to dry. When dry, dust with pink petal dusting powder.

To make the calyx for the flower, roll out a small piece of green paste into a very small Mexican hat. (The green is made up of equal quantities of Christmas and gooseberry green.) Cut out with a small 5-pointed white calyx cutter. Soften the edges and cup each sepal in the centre with a ball tool and secure to the back of the flower.

To make the buds, roll a piece of green paste into a teardrop. Moisten the end of a 26-gauge wire and insert the pointed end of the teardrop. Shape the bud to a fine point with a slender neck onto the wire. Cut twice with a sharp pair of scissors to mark the sepals. Dust with moss green dusting powder. Tape into clusters of 5–10 flowers and buds, making the stems about 4cm (1½ in) from the base of the flowers. Follow the instructions in Step 3 opposite for making the calyx. When dry, dust with moss green dusting powder.

Make the leaves as described in Step 4 opposite. Dust them with moss green dusting powder and a little nutkin brown. Using dark brown paste colouring, paint a jagged band three-quarters down the leaf in a semi-circle, as shown in the photograph of Step 4. Glaze with a half-strength glaze and allow to dry.

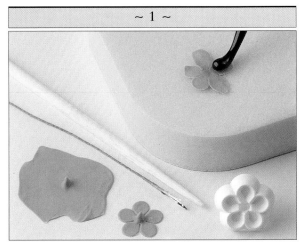

FLOWER *Using a small 5-petalled blossom cutter, cut out a shape. Place the Mexican hat into the small hole in a celpad and elongate each petal. Using ceramic veining tool, roll over each petal. Soften edges with ball tool. Insert a celstick into centre to open up throat.*

~ 3 ~

Cut out a calyx for the stem in green paste, using a sharp 6-pointed white cutter with a short Mexican hat. Soften edges of each sepal and cup with celstick. Insert celstick into throat to hollow out stem. Insert wire through centre. Secure calyx below taped flowers and buds.

~ 2 ~

Using mulberry paste colouring, paint fine lines on centre of each petal. Insert wire through centre of flower. Moisten base of stamens and secure to wire. For second layer repeat , using a slightly larger blossom cutter. Insert stamens in centre of layer and secure to flower.

~ ❖ ~

Wire up the leaves to the clusters of flowers to form a well-balanced plant.

Cutters for Geranium flower

Calyx for flower

Calyx for stem

~ 4 ~

***LEAVES** Roll out green paste on a grooved board, embedding a 26-gauge wire as described before. Cut out with different sizes of geranium leaf cutter. Vein using a geranium leaf veiner. Soften edges and allow to dry.*

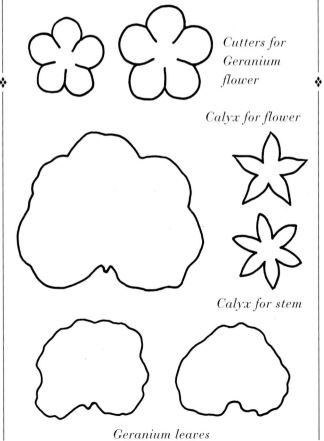

Geranium leaves

~ 1 ~

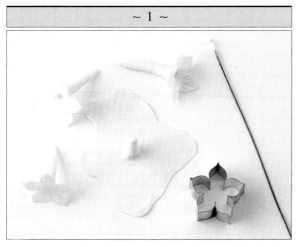

FLOWER Place shape in the medium hole of a celpad and soften edges, veining centre of each petal with veining tool. On either side of centre vein, ray out shorter veins. Press rounded end of a small celstick into centre to open up throat.

NICOTIANA

● To make a flower, first secure 6 fine white stamens to a 26-gauge wire, either with a gluegun or with floristry tape. Paint one stamen green to represent the pistil. Paint the tips of the stamens with black paste colouring. Using very pale melon flower paste, roll out a Mexican hat with a long, slender stem. Cut out a shape with a small petunia cutter. Follow the instructions in Step 1.

● Then place flower on celpad with back facing up and cup each petal lightly in the centre. Moisten base of stamens and thread wire through the flower so stamens are just below surface of petals. Secure onto wire. Vein the stem down the neck with the veining tool.

● Dust the edges of the petals, back and front, with either pale primrose dusting powder or

~ 2 ~

CALYX Roll out piece of mid green paste and cut out a very small calyx (see template on page 30). Soften edges of sepals and vein down centre of each one with a veining tool. Moisten base of stem, thread wire through centre of calyx and secure.

BUD To shape a half-open bud, pull whole floret through the large hole of the celpad. Dust to match flowers.

equal quantities of plum and burgundy. Dust the stem with pale moss green dusting powder. Tape each stem with Nile green stemtex.

● To make a bud, roll a small piece of green paste into a teardrop. Insert a moistened wire into the pointed end of the teardrop and secure onto the wire. Roll out a small piece of green paste into a Mexican hat and cut out a calyx, using a tiny calyx cutter. Soften the edges of the sepals and vein the centre of each one, using a veining tool. Thread the stem of the small bud through the centre of the calyx, moisten the bud and wrap the calyx around the bud. When dry, dust with moss green dusting powder.

● To make a half-open bud, colour flower paste with melon paste colouring to a pale cream. Roll out a piece of paste into a long, slender tube. Cut out a small blossom shape and thread the tube into the medium hole of a celpad. Elongate the tip of each petal with a dogbone tool and vein down the centre of each one with a veining tool. Thread a moistened 26-gauge wire through the centre and secure.

● Make a calyx in the same way as for a flower, see opposite.

● Use flower paste coloured with 2 parts of gooseberry green and 1 part Christmas green paste colouring for the leaves. Roll out a piece of paste over a grooved board and cut out with a leaf cutter or template, see page 30. Follow the instructions in Steps 1 and 2 right.

~ 1 ~

LEAVES *Insert a 26-gauge wire into leaf in the ridge. Vein leaves and soften edges. Allow to dry.*

~ 2 ~

Paint centre veining of leaves with an equal quantity of bitter lemon, cream and white colourings. Dust edges of leaves with primrose dusting powder, then moss green. Varnish leaves with a half-strength glaze.

~ ❖ ~

Wire flowers into irregular clusters using a selection of buds and flowers with smaller leaves interspersed between them. Then add larger leaves to bottoms of stems. Tape into an attractive plant shape and neaten base of stems, making sure they will fit into a posy pick.

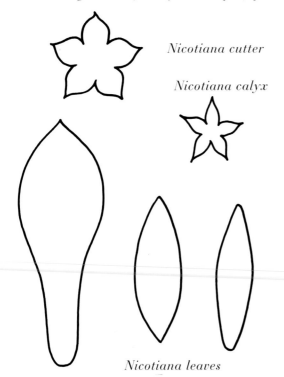

Nicotiana cutter

Nicotiana calyx

Nicotiana leaves

LOBELIA

❖

● To make the flower, roll a piece of white flower paste over a fine groove in a grooved board. Cut out the shape using a lobelia cutter. Insert a 30-gauge green wire. With a fine pair of scissors cut out a small petal from the bottom edge of the 2 outer petals. Place on a board and using a celstick, elongate the 2 fine petals. Follow the instructions in Step 1 opposite.

● The method is the same for the blue lobelia but colour the paste with 2 parts blueberry and 1 part mulberry paste colourings. Dust the petals while wet using deep purple dusting powder. Paint 2 white lines at the junction of the 3 larger petals.

● The calyx for the flower is made in exactly the same way as for the bud, see photograph of Step 2 opposite.

● To make the buds, roll a tiny piece of flower paste onto a 30-gauge green wire. Pinch the paste 5 times along its length with a pair of cranked tweezers. Bend the tips of the buds upwards. Dust the blue lobelia with a deep purple dusting powder and the white one with spring green. To create minute buds, attach the fringed stemtex tape, as used for the calyx, directly onto the end of a 30-gauge wire and trim.

● To make the calyx, follow the instructions in Step 2 opposite.

● To make leaves, cut a long, slender leaf shape from green stemtex and place on a celpad. Vein down centre using a veining tool.

~ 1 ~

Using a Dresden tool, gently frill edges of the 3 larger petals and lightly vein centre of each one. Where the wire is inserted into flower, gently wrap paste around to form a throat. Arrange the 2 fine petals vertically.

~ 2 ~

Cut a piece of dark green stemtex into 3 with a large pair of scissors. Each cut should be about 4cm (1½ in) deep. Then cut each one into 5, trimming into fine points if they appear too blunt. Attach to wire below bud.

~ ❖ ~

Wire flowers and 2–3 buds onto a 24-gauge green wire, adding a leaf where they join. Build up a spray gradually, with clusters of flowers, leaves and buds.

Lobelia trails downwards over the edge of the terracotta containers, then some strands are bent back upwards.

DIANTHUS CHRISTENING CAKE

25cm (10 in) elliptical cake
apricot glaze
875 g (1¾ lb) marzipan (almond paste)
clear alcohol (gin or vodka)
1.25kg (2½ lb) shell pink sugarpaste
Royal Icing, see page 6
pink dusting powder (petal dust/blossom tint)

EQUIPMENT

35cm (14 in) elliptical cake board
ceramic veining tool
greaseproof paper (parchment)
scriber
1m (1 yd 3 in) ribbon, 3mm (⅛ in) wide
cellophane
sheet of perspex
masking tape
no. 0 piping tube (tip)
1m (1 yd 3 in) ribbon to trim board

FLOWERS AND DECORATION

6 open dianthus flowers, see page 34
5 dianthus buds, see page 34
9 leaves, see page 35
pram

● Brush the cake with apricot glaze and cover with marzipan. Allow to dry. Brush the board with clear alcohol and cover with sugarpaste.

Using a ceramic veining tool, create a fabric effect around the outer edge of the cake board. Allow to dry. Brush the cake with clear alcohol and cover with sugarpaste. When dry, place the cake on the board.

● Measure the height and circumference of the cake and make a greaseproof paper template by folding the paper into 4 equal sections. Trace the design, see page 70. Pin the template to the side of the cake and scribe the curved line. Remove the template and then attach narrow ribbon to the base of the cake, covering the join with a tiny bow.

● Stick cellophane to a sheet of perspex with masking tape. Using white royal icing and a no. 0 tube, pipe the lace pieces, using template on this page. Allow to dry. Tint the edges of the lace pieces with pink dusting powder. Carefully remove the pieces from the cellophane and attach to the scribed line on the cake with dots of royal icing. Stick the ribbon to the edge of the board.

● Using the template for the path on page 35, roll and cut out 9 pebbles in pale melon flower paste.

● Stick the pebbles onto the top of the cake, as shown in the photograph. Position the pram and the bunch of dianthus, securing with dots of royal icing. Finally, pipe the baby's name.

Lace piece

Dianthus cutter with cuts shown

Sepal

Leaves

DIANTHUS

❖

● Using pale pink flower paste, roll a long-stemmed Mexican hat and cut out a circle with a 2cm (¾ in) round cutter. Follow the instructions in Steps 1 and 2 on this page.

● Using ruby paste food colouring, paint a jagged circle around the inner rim, as shown in the photograph of Step 2. Dust the outer edge with pink dusting powder.

● Roll out silvery green flower paste and cut out a sepal, using a small calyx cutter. Cut into sections, see diagram on page 32. Place on a pad and soften the edges with a ball tool. Moisten the stem and secure sepals around. Allow to dry.

● To make a bud, roll a piece of pale pink flower paste into a ball and place on a 26-gauge green wire. Roll into a cigar shape and thin into

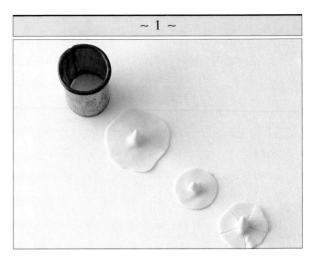

~ 1 ~

Use a craft knife to cut circle into 5 equal sections, see diagram on page 32. Flute each petal using a Dresden tool and a little cornflour (cornstarch).

~ 2 ~

Insert a celstick into centre to open up throat, then push in a 26-gauge wire and secure. Cut heads off 2 fine silk stamens, then curl these lightly using a pair of scissors and insert in centre of flower.

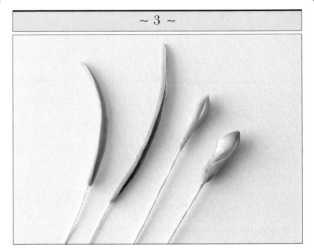

~ 3 ~

BUDS AND LEAVES Insert a 28-gauge wire in ridge. Place on a pad, soften edges and mark a vein down centre. Place on a piece of foam sponge to dry, then dust with pale moss green dusting powder.

a long stem, see photograph of Step 3 opposite. Dust with pink dusting powder. Make a calyx as for open dianthus.

● To make a leaf, roll out a strip of silvery green flower paste, leaving a ridge on the end. Cut out a thin strip with a craft knife, see template on page 32. Follow the instructions in Step 3 opposite.

● Arrange the flowers, buds and leaves into a bunch.

PRAM

❖

● Roll out pale pink flower paste and cut out 2 3.5cm (1½ in) and 2 2.5cm (1 in) wheels using round cutters or the templates below. Follow the instructions in Steps 1, 2 and 3 on page 36.

● Curve the base around the edge of the side template and allow to dry in this position, using pieces of foam sponge as supports.

● Roll out 3 thin, round matchstick-sized pieces of pale pink flower paste for the handle. Leave one straight and bend the other 2 into 'S' shapes, see diagram below. Allow to dry. Brush all the fluted edges with pink dusting powder.

● Using a no. 1 tube and pale pink royal icing, pipe a line around the outer bottom edge of one pram side and secure to the curved base. Pipe a line along the other edge of the base and attach the second side. Allow to dry.

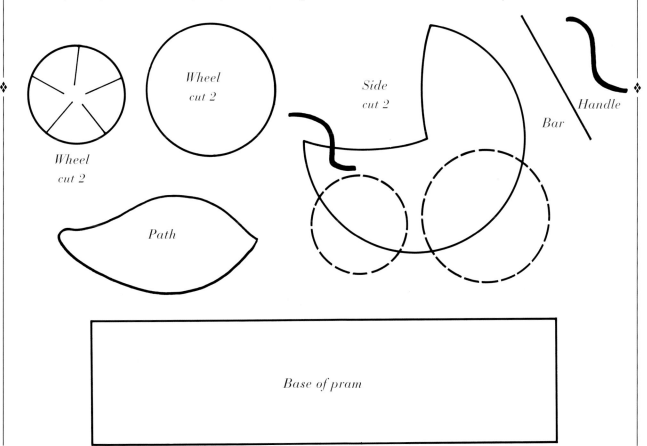

Wheel
cut 2

Wheel
cut 2

Path

Side
cut 2

Bar

Handle

Base of pram

Secure one of the small wheels to the front of the pram with dots of royal icing, then one of the large ones to the back and also one of the handles to the side, see diagram on page 35. Allow to dry, then repeat on the other side of the pram. Allow to dry again, then attach the straight handle, supporting it with a piece of foam sponge until dry.

EXPERT ADVICE

≈

Using a piece of absorbent kitchen paper, smear a minute amount of white vegetable fat (shortening) onto the cellophane. This will help when removing the lace.

1

Make 5 equal cuts into each wheel as shown and flute the edges, using a Dresden tool and a little cornflour (cornstarch). Allow to dry. Paint a jagged circle around centre of wheels, using ruby paste food colouring.

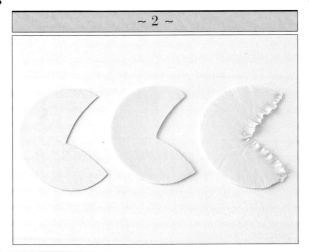

Using template on page 35, roll and cut out sides of pram. Flute the 2 inner edges of each side and leave to dry.

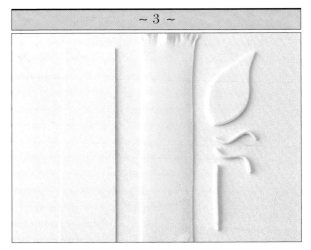

Using template on page 35, roll and cut out base of pram. Flute the 2 narrow ends with a Dresden tool. Path and pram handles pieces also shown on the right.

CASABLANCA FANTASY WEDDING CAKE

35cm (14 in) teardrop cake
30cm (12 in) teardrop cake
25cm (10 in) teardrop cake
apricot glaze
3.75kg (7½ lb) marzipan (almond paste)
clear alcohol (gin or vodka)
4.5kg (9 lb) pale mint green sugarpaste
1½ tsp gum tragacanth
750g (1½ lb) ivory sugarpaste

EQUIPMENT

45cm (18 in) oval board
38cm (15 in) teardrop board
33cm (13 in) teardrop board
greaseproof paper (parchment)
no. 2 piping tube (tip)
3.25m (3½ yd) feather-edged ivory ribbon
white plastic dowels
3 wilton double-ended crystal pillars, 13cm
(5 in) high, cut in half
cel non-slip matting for texturing

FLOWERS

24 open Solomon's seal, see page 38
27 Solomon's seal buds, see page 38
24 Solomon's seal leaves, various sizes,
see page 38
5 open Casablanca lilies, see page 40
1 half-open Casablanca lily, see page 40
2 Casablanca buds, see page 40
8 lily leaves, see page 40
1 open cream rose, see page 42
2 three-quarter-open cream roses, see page 42
4 half-open cream roses, see page 42
6 large rosebuds, see page 42
10 tight rosebuds, see page 42
17 large ivy leaves, see page 44
25 medium ivy leaves, see page 44
30 small ivy leaves, see page 44

● Brush the cakes with apricot glaze and cover with marzipan. Allow to dry. Brush the cakes and boards with clear alcohol and cover with pale mint green sugarpaste. When dry, place the cakes on the boards.

● Soften some of the pale mint green sugarpaste with sufficient warm, boiled water to

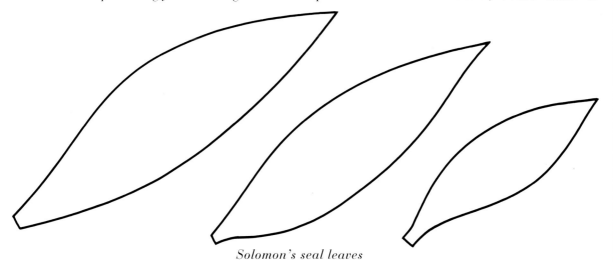

Solomon's seal leaves

make a piping consistency. Allow to cool. Using a no. 2 tube, pipe a fine snail's trail around the base of each cake, joining the cakes to the board. Set aside to dry. Attach feather-edged ribbon around each board.

Make a paper template of each cake tin and use these to mark the positions of the pillars on the cakes, see the diagram on page 71. Use white plastic dowels in the cakes as these will show less through the crystal pillars than the ordinary wooden dowelling would. Alternatively, the exposed portions of the dowels could be covered with the same ribbon used for edging the boards; if so, allow for this when buying the ribbon.

Knead the gum tragacanth into the ivory sugarpaste to make a modelling paste and leave to mature for 12 hours. Measure the length of the paste required to make each drape and cut a piece of greaseproof paper of this length. Fold the greaseproof paper as you will require it for the drapes and use as templates.

Roll out the modelling paste and texture it with the non-slip matting. Cut out the drapes one at a time. Moisten the surface of the cake with clear alcohol and attach the drapes in position, adjusting the folds attractively. Repeat this for each tier.

To make the decorative braiding, roll 3 long sausages of modelling paste, moisten them lightly so they stick together and then twist into a decorative rope. Finish the upper edge of each drape with this decoration.

Wire the flowers and leaves together and position as shown in the photograph.

Detail of drape

SOLOMON'S SEAL

Using a glue gun, glue 6 tiny pale lemon silk stamens and 1 white pistil onto a 32-gauge pale green wire. Roll a small ball of white flower paste into a teardrop. Follow the instructions in Steps 1 and 2 on page 40.

Insert the stamen wire through the centre of the flower and secure. Allow to dry. Dust the petals with equal quantities of moss green and primrose dusting powders.

To make the buds, roll a piece of white flower paste into a teardrop shape. Insert a 32-gauge pale green wire into the pointed end and secure. With a fine pair of scissors, make 3 cuts into the broad end and allow to dry. Dust with the same mixture of dusting powders used on the flowers. Keep some buds separate and wire the remaining buds and flowers together into pairs.

To make the leaves, colour some flower paste with 2 parts Christmas green and 2 parts gooseberry green colouring. Roll out a piece of the green paste onto a grooved board. Using the

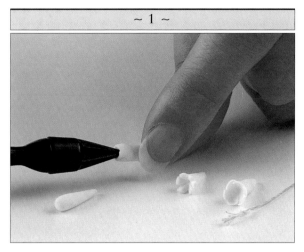

~ 1 ~

Dip a 6-pointed veining tool into white vegetable fat (shortening) and then about 3mm (⅛ in) into large end of teardrop to divide paste into 6 equal parts. Cut with fine pointed scissors. Separate petals and ball out using a small celstick on a pad.

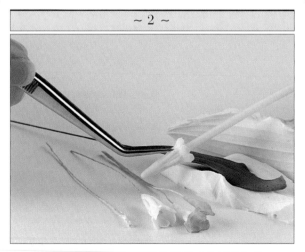

~ 2 ~

Insert a small celstick into centre of flower, leaving it in place. Using long-nosed, cranked tweezers, pinch down back of flower between petals. Gently removing celstick, arrange 3 petals towards centre and remaining 3 petals to outside.

templates on page 37, cut out leaves in various sizes. Insert a 26-gauge green wire in each leaf and vein with a Solomon's seal leaf veiner, then soften the edges. Allow to dry. Dust the leaves using 2 parts moss green to 1 part apple green dusting powder. Use half-strength glaze to glaze the leaves.

● Begin forming the Solomon's seal into its sprays by wiring a small leaf to the tip of an 18-gauge wire. Add 2 more small leaves and then begin wiring in the buds and flowers, starting with a single bud wired in below a leaf, then a pair of buds to a leaf and finally mixed pairs of buds and flowers to each leaf. The leaves are wired in alternate formation and become larger towards the bottom of the stem. Strengthen the stem by adding further 18-gauge wires as necessary. Check that the flowers are hanging neatly below the leaves and curve the sprays attractively.

CASABLANCA LILY

● First make the stamens. Cut 2 26-gauge white wires into 3. Strip a piece of white stemtex into quarters. Bind the 6 wires in sequence of quarter of the way up the wire, half way up, three-quarters of the way up and finally all the way up. Bend the thinner end of each wire to an angle as shown in the photograph of Step 1 opposite. Roll pieces of pale green flower paste into small cigar shapes. Follow the instructions in Step 1 opposite.

● For the pistil, roll a piece of light green flower paste into a teardrop shape. Insert a 22-gauge wire and roll the paste down the stem about 7cm (2¾ in). Shape the stem of the pistil by curving it gently. Pinch the top of the stem into a triangular shape. Roll a small piece of

~ 1 ~

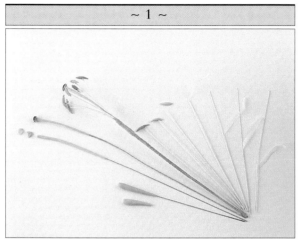

Moisten bent end of each wire and insert into back of cigar shape, bending paste over to form bridge shape. Moisten ends of stamens and dip into semolina coloured with tangerine and skintone dusting powders.

~ 2 ~

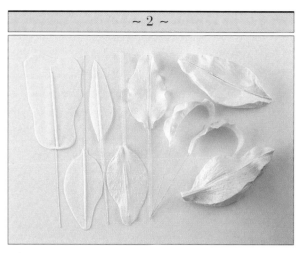

Place petal in between a double-sided Casablanca lily veiner. Remove from veiner and frill edges on a pad. Bend wire over to shape petal.

~ 3 ~

Using veining tool, vein twice down each ridge to divide into 2 parts, also vein centre of bud. Dust with spring green dusting powder and allow to dry. Wire buds onto 2 more 18-gauge wires.

~ 4 ~

Using lily leaf cutters or templates on page 45, cut out shape and vein using lily leaf veiner. Soften edges and allow to dry. Dust with moss green and a little primrose yellow dusting powders. Glaze with half-strength glaze.

green paste into a ball. Place on a pad and flatten with a celstick. Shape into 3, see diagram on page 45. Moisten the end of the pistil and attach this to form a little hat. Divide into 3 with a craft knife and leave to dry. Moisten the end of the pistil and dip into aubergine dusting powder. Wire the stamens around the base of the pistil, see the photograph of Step 1 on page 41.

To make the petals, roll out a piece of white flower paste over a grooved board, laying a 24-gauge white wire over the groove and rolling it into the paste. Cut out the petal using a large Casablanca lily cutter or a template, see page 45. Follow the instructions in Step 2 on page 41.

Place the petal on a piece of foam sponge to help to keep the shape. While the petal is drying, roll out 2 more petals in the same way. Using the narrow cutter from the Casablanca set or the template on page 45, cut 3 more petals. Repeat the veining and shaping as for the broader petals.

While the petals are still slightly damp, dust the base and the centre vein at the back of each petal with spring green dusting powder. Wire the 3 large petals around the pistil and stamens, then add the narrow petals to the back in between the large petals. Secure stems to an 18-gauge wire and tape stems down.

To make the buds, first bend a hook in an 18-gauge wire. Roll a large ball of flower paste into a cigar shape, pinching down the paste to divide into 3 equal sections. Place on an 18-gauge wire and secure. Follow the instructions in Step 3 on page 41.

The open bud is made in the same way as the open lily except that the stamens are left straight and the petals are not bent back.

To make the leaves, roll out a piece of spruce green paste over a grooved board. Place a 26-gauge wire on top of the groove and roll the wire into the paste. Follow the instructions in Step 4 on page 41.

ROSES AND ROSEBUDS

Start by making a tight rosebud. Roll a piece of white flower paste into a cone shape. Bend a hook in an 18-gauge wire. Moisten and insert into the cone and allow to dry. Roll out a piece of cream coloured flower paste and cut out a single petal. Soften the edges and vein with a rose veiner. Moisten the petal and wrap this around the cone. Allow to dry. Make a calyx as described opposite.

Moisten the base of the cone and insert the wire through the centre of the calyx and secure

ROSEBUD Wrap a single veined petal around the cone. Allow to dry, then secure the calyx tightly around the bud as shown.

~ 1 ~

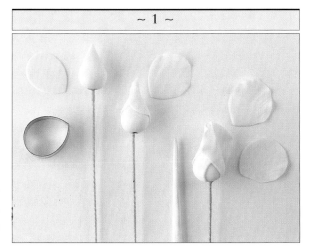

Wrap one side of first petal around cone and tuck second one into this, wrapping both around cone as shown. At this stage if a calyx were added, it could be used as a slightly opened bud.

~ 2 ~

Turning petals over, cup centre of each one and insert a moistened wire into thickened point. Allow to dry in a cupped position. This may be used as an open rose.

tightly around the bud. Dust the calyx with moss green dusting powder and the tips with aubergine.

To make a rose and opened buds, bend a hook in an 18-gauge wire. Roll a piece of ivory coloured flower paste into a cone shape and place on the wire. Roll out a piece of ivory flower paste and cut out a petal, using the smaller of the cutters, see diagram on page 45. Vein the petal with a ceramic veining tool and soften the edges. Moisten all over and secure to the cone. Cut out 2 more petals and vein with the ceramic veining tool. Soften the edges. Follow the instructions in Step 1 above.

Roll out another piece of flower paste and cut out 2 more petals. Repeat as for the previous layer. Once again if a calyx were added, you would have a slightly larger bud.

Roll out another piece of flower paste and

~ ❖ ~

CALYX Roll out a piece of spruce green flower paste into a very small Mexican hat. Cut out calyx, using a suitable-sized calyx cutter. Elongate each sepal and cut down both sides of 3 of the sepals. Place on pad and soften edges.

using a slightly larger cutter, cut out 2 more petals. Vein each petal with the ceramic veining tool. Place on a pad and soften the edges. Turning the petals over and cupping the back of each petal, moisten a 'V' at the base of each petal and secure these around the cone. See the photograph of Step 2 on page 43. Be careful not to remove the cupping by pushing. This may also be used as a slightly opened rose.

● Roll out another piece of paste. Cut out 3 petals, using the same sized cutter. Vein each petal, using the ceramic veining tool. Place the petals on a pad and soften the edges. Turning each petal over, cup as for the previous layer, bending the petals back slightly. Secure each petal around the cone.

● Bend a small hook into 5 28-gauge white wires. Roll out a piece of flower paste, leaving a ridge at the edge. Using a slightly larger cutter, cut out 5 petals with the ridge at the base of each petal. Vein each petal with the ceramic veining tool. Placing each petal on a pad, soften the edges. Follow Step 2 on page 43.

● Cut out 5 more petals and repeat the process as before.

● Roll out a piece of spruce green flower paste into a small Mexican hat. Using a large calyx cutter, cut out the calyx. Elongate each sepal and cut down both sides of 3 of the sepals with a pair of scissors. Place the calyx on the celpad and soften the edges. Vein down the centre of each sepal with a veining tool and cup the sepals backwards with a ball tool. Moisten the centre of the calyx and thread the wire through the centre. Position the sepals at the joins between the petals. Dust the calyx on the back with moss green dusting powder. Brush the tips of the sepals with aubergine dusting powder. It is best to do so before calyx is dry.

Ivy Insert a 26-gauge green wire. Vein leaf with an ivy veiner, soften edges and allow to dry. Dust leaf with forest green dusting powder and edges with nutkin brown. Use half-strength glaze to glaze.

IVY

Colour flower paste with spruce green paste colouring to form a dark green. Roll out the paste onto a grooved board. Cut out leaves in different sizes using ivy cutters or templates (see page 70). Follow the instructions given above and on page 10 for general leaf-making instructions.

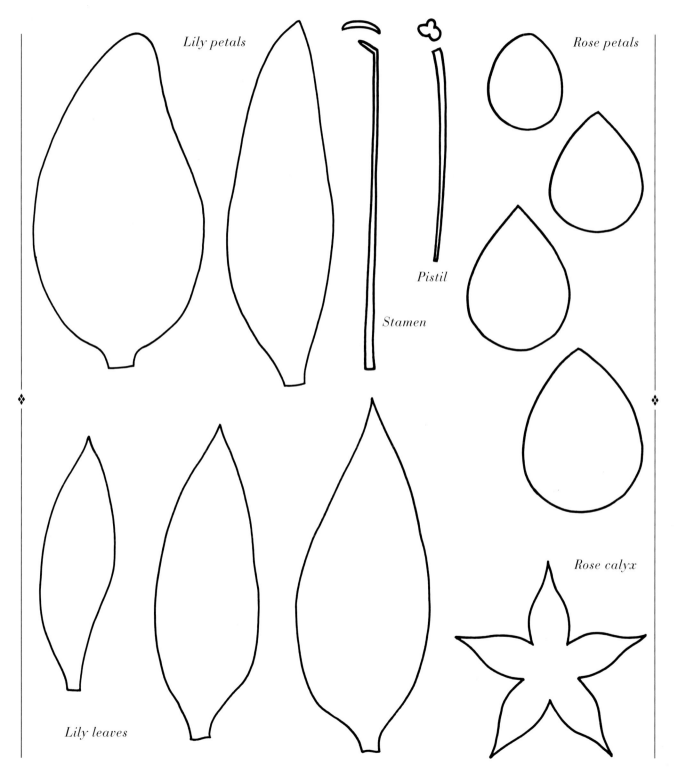

Lily petals

Rose petals

Pistil

Stamen

Rose calyx

Lily leaves

GOLDEN WEDDING CAKE

25cm (10 in) scalloped oval cake with another
scallop cut into the front
apricot glaze
1kg (2 lb) marzipan (almond paste)
clear alcohol (gin or vodka)
1kg (2 lb) ivory sugarpaste
375g (12 oz) egg yellow sugarpaste
Royal Icing, see page 6

EQUIPMENT

33cm (13 in) oval cake board
embossed plastic table cloth
90cm (1 yd) ribbon, 3mm (⅛ in) wide
greaseproof paper (parchment)
no. 1 piping tube (tip)
1.05m (1 yd 6 in) ribbon to trim board
double-sided adhesive tape
posy pick

FLOWERS

1 large open sunflower, see this page
1 small sunflower bud, see this page
7 tea rose buds, see page 50
5 open tea roses, see page 50
7 rose leaf stems, see page 50
5 large ivy leaf stems, see page 50

● This cake is ideal for a summer celebration of a golden wedding.

● Brush the cake with apricot glaze and cover with marzipan and allow to dry. Brush the cake with clear alcohol, cover with ivory sugarpaste and allow to dry.

● Brush the board with clear alcohol and cover with egg yellow sugarpaste. Place the embossed plastic table cloth over the cake board, and press over with a cake smoother. Remove the cloth and allow to dry.

● Place the cake on the board and wrap 2 bands of 3mm (⅛ in) wide ribbon around the cake, securing with dots of royal icing.

● Using a no. 1 tube, pipe an ivory border around the base of the cake.

● Secure ribbon around the edge of the board, using double-sided adhesive tape. Insert the spray into the cake, using a posy pick.

SUNFLOWER

● Roll a large piece of dark brown flower paste into a ball and flatten, hollowing out the centre. Bend a hook on an 18-gauge wire and then bend horizontally. Follow the instructions in Steps 1 and 2 on page 48.

● Turn the petals over and cup the back of each one. Turn petals over again, place on a piece of absorbent kitchen paper and dust with lemon and then egg yellow dusting powders. Moisten the centre of the flower and secure to cone. Repeat this twice. Then make the calyx, see Step 3 on page 48.

● It may be necessary to hang the flower upside down to dry. Tape another 2 18-gauge wires to the stem for strength.

● For the buds, make the centre as for the flower but smaller. Roll out a piece of egg yellow flower paste and using a smaller cutter, cut out petals. Place on a pad, soften the edges

---

EXPERT ADVICE

≈

To achieve an accurate cut when using a large cutter, roll out flower paste, lay over the top of the cutter and roll over with a rolling pin.

Rose petal

Rose calyx

~ 1 ~

Moisten wire and insert into back of cone as shown. Moisten front of cone and dip into rolled oats or semolina coloured with nutkin brown dusting powder. Dust outer edge with lemon dusting powder and allow to dry.

~ 2 ~

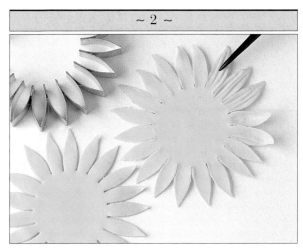

Roll out a large piece of egg yellow flower paste and using a sunflower cutter, cut out shape. Place on a pad and soften edges with a ball tool. Using a Dresden veining tool, vein each petal vertically.

~ 3 ~

Roll out a piece of Christmas green flower paste. Cut out a calyx, using a chrysanthemum petal cutter, and place on a pad. Soften edges and cup. Moisten and secure to base of flower. Repeat twice and allow to dry. Dust with moss green dusting powder.

~ 4 ~

LEAVES Vein and soften edges, then allow to dry. Dust leaves with moss green and lemon dusting powders. Use half-strength glaze to glaze leaves.

and vein using a Dresden tool. Place on a piece of absorbent kitchen paper and dust with lemon and then egg yellow dusting powders. Moisten the centre and secure to the base. Wrap the petals around the base and repeat once more. Repeat calyx as for the flower. Add another 2 18-gauge wires for strength.

● For the leaves, colour a piece of flower paste with equal quantities of Christmas green and gooseberry green paste colourings and roll out over a grooved board, see page 10. Insert a 24-gauge wire and cut out leaves, using template on page 70. Follow the instructions in Step 4 opposite.

Sunflower calyx
(2 sizes shown)

Sunflower

Sunflower

TEA ROSE

❖

◯ Follow the instructions in Step 1 opposite. Then place a cone of flower paste on a hooked 20-gauge wire. Moisten the whole of one petal, insert the wire through the centre and secure this petal firmly around the cone. Moisten the sides only of the second and third petals. Then follow the instructions in Step 2 opposite.

◯ Cut out a further shape for the second layer. Vein and soften edges. Turn the petals over and cup the centre of each one as shown in step 1. Then follow the instructions in Step 3 opposite.

◯ Continue around the flower, bending the petals back as you go. Allow to dry.

◯ For the buds, follow the instructions for the tea rose using only one layer of petals. Leave the two outer petals slightly open. Allow to dry. Dust the open rose and buds with lemon and egg yellow, then the outer edges with plum.

◯ For the calyx, using a smaller cutter, follow the instructions for the rose calyx on the Casablanca Fantasy Wedding Cake, see page 42.

◯ For the leaves, colour a piece of flower paste with equal quantities of Christmas green and spruce green paste colourings and roll out over a grooved board. Follow the instructions in Step 4 opposite. Dust the leaves with red, moss green, lemon and jade dusting powders. Glaze with half-strength glaze. For each stem you will need 1 large, 2 medium and 2 small leaves.

◯ When wiring the leaves, use quarter-width brown floristry tape for the ivy leaves and Nile green floristry tape for the rose leaves. The stem of ivy may vary in length depending on the size of your spray. Bend stem and leaves for a more natural look. Follow the instructions in Steps 5 and 6 opposite.

~ 1 ~

Roll out a piece of pale egg yellow flower paste and using a medium size 5-petalled blossom cutter, cut out shape. Vein using a ceramic veining tool. Soften edges.

~ 4 ~

Cut out leaves with a rose leaf cutter and insert a moistened 28-gauge wire into groove. Vein with a rose leaf veiner, then place on a pad and soften edges. Allow to dry.

~ 2 ~

Wrap second petal halfway around cone and tuck third into second and wrap around, making sure they are slightly higher than first petal. Moisten sides of fourth and fifth petals and repeat as for second and third.

~ 3 ~

Moisten sides of first petal, insert wire through the centre and secure petal so it covers gap in first layer, bending side edges of petals back with a cocktail stick (toothpick).

~ 5 ~

LEAVES Twist brown tape into a tendril with a cocktail stick. Attach to a small ivy leaf (see page 44), adding a 20-gauge wire and a medium leaf to stem and then a larger leaf. Tape a 24-gauge wire to large rose leaf, then add 2 medium leaves and then 2 smaller ones.

~ 6 ~

Tape 2 stems of rose leaves and 1 stem of ivy together and add 2 rose buds and one open bud. You will need 6 of these sprays.

MAKING THE SPRAY

Tape together the sunflower and bud, being extra careful not to knock the petals. Add the sunflower leaves, then the sprays of roses and ivy, bending the stems to an 'L' shape to fit the stem. There are 4 sprays in the top section and 2 in the bottom. The photograph on the right shows the back of the finished spray.

EXPERT ADVICE
≈

If you find you have a gap when wiring you may be able to fill it with extra leaves.

The back of the spray

The finished spray

CANDLESTICK CRESCENT

1 pottery candlestick
Nile green floristry tape
24-gauge white wires
glue gun
small yellow hammerhead stamens
selection of dusting powders (petal dusts/blossom tints)
flower paste
30-gauge white and green wires
flat Christmas rose petal veiner
ceramic silk veining tool
dimpled foam sponge
cranked tweezers
miniature fuchsia sepal cutter
philadelphus veiner
half-strength glaze
medium cattleya orchid petal cutters
large and small sets of simple leaf cutters
28-gauge green wires
26-gauge green wires
18-gauge wire
silver floristry wire

● Measure the height and width of the candlestick. This will enable you to decide on the length of each spray of philadelphus you are using in the arrangement.

● Tape a piece of quarter-width tape onto a 24-gauge white wire, leaving about 1cm (½ in) of tape free above the top of the wire. Cut this into 3, taking fine wedges of tape from between the fine filaments.

● Using a glue gun, attach 28 stamens (14 stamens cut into 2 lengths) onto the 24-gauge wire. Make sure that the stamens are shorter in the centre and longer towards the outside. It is also very noticeable that the stamens are longer at the junction between the petals. Tape over the base of the stamens with quarter-width Nile green floristry tape. Dust to taste.

● Each flower has 4 petals. Make several different sizes of flowers so that you can graduate the flowers down the stems.

● Roll a piece of white flower paste into a sausage shape. Roll the paste away from the sausage shape until it is fine, but leave a thickened section. Using the template below, place on the rolled-out paste with the point on

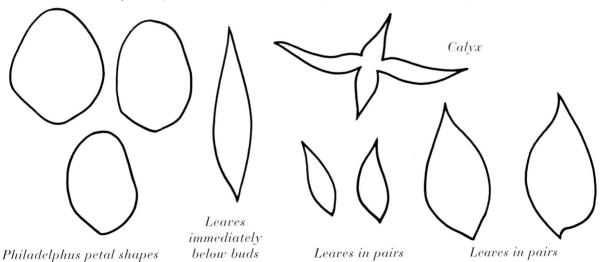

Calyx

Philadelphus petal shapes

Leaves immediately below buds

Leaves in pairs

Leaves in pairs

the thicker section. Cut out 4 petals. Make a small hook at the end of a quarter-length 30-gauge wire. Moisten and insert the hooked end of the wire into the thickened part of the paste. Follow the instructions in Step 1 on page 56.

Place the petals on dimpled foam sponge to curve into shape. When they have dried to the leather-hard stage, dust each base with a mixture of plum, burgundy and aubergine dusting powders.

Darken the tips of the stamens with a little lemon and egg yellow dusting powders. Using a pair of cranked tweezers, curve the stamens very slightly. Using a quarter-width piece of Nile green floristry tape, attach the 4 petals in 2 pairs immediately below the stamens.

Make a small Mexican hat of mid-green flower paste. Roll out the paste from the centre and placing the fuchsia sepal cutter over the Mexican hat, cut out a shape. Remove the cutter. Place the sepals on the board. The sepals are unequal in size, 2 being much longer than the others; elongate 2 opposite sepals. Soften the edges on foam sponge. Using a philadelphus veiner, mark a vein down the centre of each sepal. Follow the instructions in Step 2 on page 56.

Dust the calyx with a little yellow dusting powder and moss green and a little forest green on the edges of the sepals. Make 18 philadelphus flowers.

For a more mature flower, make a longish cone of pale green paste and attach this in the centre of the stamens. The petals on the mature flowers are almost flat.

To make the bracts, use the cattleya orchid petal cutters to cut out 2 shapes from mid-green flower paste. Insert 28-gauge green wire into the centre of these shapes and carefully vein down the centre. Soften the edges on a foam sponge. Pinch the tip of the bract together and curve backwards. Allow to set in a curve. Dust with forest green, moss green and a little nutkin brown dusting powders. Glaze with half-strength glaze. The bracts are attached immediately behind the flowers.

For the bud, make a small cone of white paste. Make a 4-wired cage and mark the bud with the cage. Make the calyx as for the flower but close it against the sides of the bud. Make 6 buds.

Make 108 leaves of various sizes, including tiny ones which form the tips of the stems. Using the templates on page 53 or simple leaf cutters, cut out leaves in green flower paste. Insert a green 30-gauge wire into the centre of the smaller leaves and a 26-gauge wire for the large ones. Vein with a philadelphus veiner. Dust the smaller leaves with apple and moss green dusting powders and glaze with half-strength glaze. Follow the instructions in Step 3 on page 56 for the larger leaves.

To assemble the philadelphus, start the stem with a number of small leaves wired onto an 18-gauge wire. The leaves are in pairs and towards the tip are attached together quite closely; alternate each pair. As the leaves get larger, so does the spacing between the leaves. The flowers and buds arise from the leaf axils. Use Nile green tape to tape the flowers and leaves onto the stem and then dust to taste (see Step 4 on page 56).

Wire the component parts into an elegant crescent shape and attach to the base of the candlestick with a length of silver floristry wire. Once it is in place, rearrange the flowers and leaves.

~ 1 ~

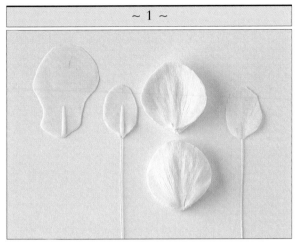

Soften edges of petals. Vein with a Christmas rose petal reiner. Frill edges of petals gently with a ceramic silk reining tool. Mark a rein strongly down centre of each petal.

~ 2 ~

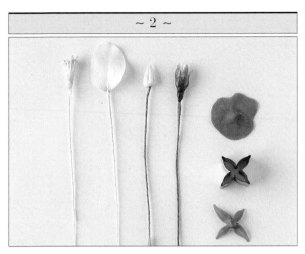

Moisten centre of sepals and attach immediately behind petals, making sure sepals fit between petals behind longer stamens.

~ 3 ~

Using a pair of curved scissors, cut slender notches into edges of larger leaves. Dust these with moss green and forest green dusting powder, using a little nutkin brown up central reins and glaze with half-strength glaze.

~ 4 ~

After the flowers and leaves have been taped onto the stem, dust to achieve the desired effect.

FUCHSIA

fine silk stamens
glue gun
28-gauge white wires
selection of paste food colourings
flower paste
small 5-petalled blossom cutter
small fuchsia cutter
celpad
celstick
selection of dusting powders (petal
dusts/blossom tints)
paintbrush
set of 3 white Japanese maple leaf cutters
double-sided fuchsia leaf veiner
30-gauge white wires
half-strength glaze
reddish brown floristry tape

Take 8 silk stamens. Use one as the pistil by making it considerably longer than the others which are arranged in various lengths. Using a glue gun, glue the stamens to a 28-gauge white wire.

Using two-thirds navy blue and one-third mulberry paste food colourings, mix flower paste to a midnight blue colour. Roll out a piece of paste and cut out a 5-petalled blossom shape. Cut off one petal, leaving 4. Follow the instructions in Step 1 on page 58.

Roll a piece of ruby coloured flower paste into a medium ball, then into a fine tube. Pinch out one end flat to form a very long, fine Mexican hat and roll out thinly. Place the fuchsia cutter over the tube and cut out a shape. Remove the cutter and elongate each sepal. Place the sepals on a celpad and soften the edges. Insert a small celstick into the centre of the tube to open. Follow the instructions in Step 2 on page 58.

To form the ovary, roll a very small ball of pale green flower paste into a cigar shape. Thread the wire through this and keep the cigar shape as you attach it to the stem just above the tube. Make 9 open fuchsias.

To make a bud, roll a piece of ruby coloured flower paste into a ball and place on a 28-gauge white wire. Roll into a cigar shape and thin into a long stem. Shape the ovary as described above for the flower. Follow the instructions in Step 3 on page 58.

Make 27 buds in various sizes. The tiny buds are made in the same way as the larger ones, but use pale green flower paste, dusting them with moss green and nutkin brown dusting powders.

Roll out a piece of pale spruce green flower

~ 1 ~

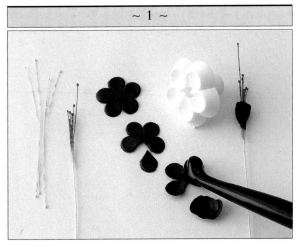

Soften edges and cup centres of each petal. Moisten edges and overlap to form a fan shape. Cup to join petals together firmly. Lay stamens in centre and wrap petals tightly around stem.

~ 2 ~

Moisten back of petals and a little of the wire, and gently insert wire through tube. Make sure tube is slender. Secure sepals against petals.

~ 3 ~

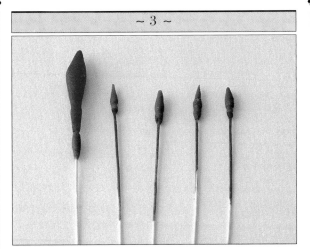

Dust ovaries with moss green and nutkin brown dusting powders. Paint stamens with ruby red paste food colouring.

~ 4 ~

Place a paste-covered wire on bottom half of a double-sided fuchsia leaf veiner with a leaflet on top of wire. Place upper half of veiner on top and press together.

paste. Using 3 sizes of Japanese maple leaf cutters, cut out 36 leaves. Dissect each leaf into 5 leaflets. Roll a small ball of flower paste onto a 30-gauge white wire, as shown in the photograph. Follow the instructions in Step 4 opposite.

Remove the leaves from the veiner and allow to dry in interesting shapes. Dust them with moss green dusting powder marking a very fine line down the centre and back of each leaf with ruby red paste food colouring. Glaze the leaves with half-strength glaze.

Wire together using reddish brown floristry tape. Start the spray with very small leaves and buds, graduating to larger ones as you go down the stem in clusters of 3 leaves and 3 buds. Dust the stems with burgundy dusting powder.

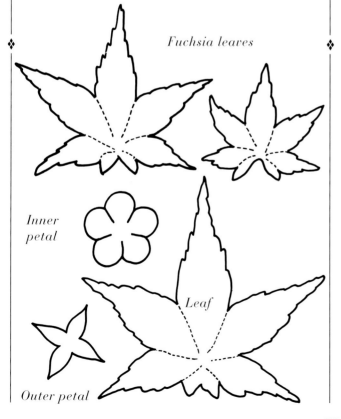

Fuchsia leaves

Inner petal

Leaf

Outer petal

SNOWDROPS

glue gun
tiny silk stamens
26-gauge green wire
selection of paste food colourings
flower paste
snowdrop cutters
celpad
ball tool
paintbrush
celstick
ceramic silk veining tool
28-gauge green wire
selection of dusting powders (petal
dusts/blossom tints)
piece of driftwood
dark brown sugarpaste

Using a glue gun, attach 6 stamens to a 26-gauge wire. Paint the stamens with tangerine paste food colouring, then allow to dry. Roll a small piece of white flower paste into a Mexican hat shape. Cut out the petals, using part 1 of the snowdrop cutters, see page 61. Place the stem in the small hole of a celpad, soften the edges and cup the centre with a ball tool. Follow the instructions in Step 1 on page 60.

Paint a small squiggle on the back of each petal, see photograph of Step 1 on page 60.

Roll out some white flower paste and cut out petals, using part 2 of the snowdrop cutters. Place on celpad and soften the edge. Follow the instructions in Step 2 on page 60.

For the ovary, roll a small piece of pale green flower paste into an oval. Moisten the base of the flower and insert the wire through the centre of the ovary, then secure. Follow the instructions in Step 3 on page 60 for making

~ 1 ~

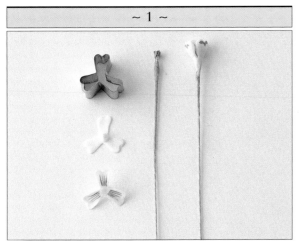

Using Christmas green food paste colouring, paint vertical lines on inside of each petal. Insert a small celstick into centre to open up throat. Moisten base of stamens and insert wire through centre. Secure and allow to dry.

~ 2 ~

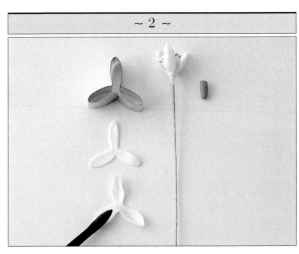

Vein down the centre of each petal with a reiner. Using a ball tool, lightly draw from the outer edge inwards. Moisten the centre and insert the wire, securing the petals in between the first petals. Allow to dry.

~ 3 ~

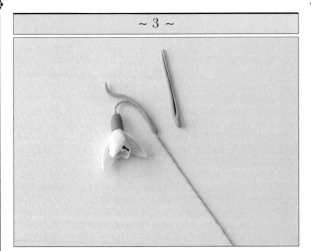

Roll a long thin piece of pale green flower paste, place on a pad and vein down centre with a veining tool. Bend head of the snowdrop over and attach bract to back of stem.

~ 4 ~

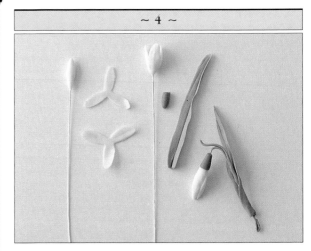

Moisten cone, insert wire through centre of petals and secure around cone. Add ovary and bract for open snowdrop.

the bract. Make at least 18 open snowdrops.

● For the snowdrop bud, roll a small oval cone of white flower paste and secure to a 26-gauge wire. Allow to dry. Roll out white flower paste and cut out using part 2 of the cutter. Place on a pad, soften the edges, then vein down the centre of each petal. With a ball tool, lightly draw from the outer edge inwards. Follow the instructions in Step 4 opposite. Make 3 snowdrop buds.

● Roll out a strip of pale green flower paste for the leaf, leaving a ridge on the end. Using the template below, cut out with a craft knife. Insert a 28-gauge wire into the ridge, place on a pad, soften the edges and vein down the centre. Place on a piece of foam sponge to dry. Dust with 2 parts white, 1 part navy blue and 2 parts moss green dusting powders.

● Find a suitable crevice in a piece of driftwood and insert a piece of dark brown sugarpaste. Arrange the snowdrops. If liked, decorate the base of the stems with autumn-coloured leaves.

EXPERT ADVICE

≈

To prevent the flowers from twisting while they are being arranged in the driftwood, bend over the ends of the stems.

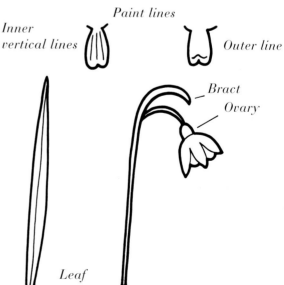

Inner vertical lines   *Paint lines*   *Outer line*

Bract
Ovary

Part 1 cutter

Part 2 cutter

Leaf

PEONY

80-gauge white cotton thread
celstick
30-gauge white wires
egg white
scriber
flower paste
selection of paste food colourings
18-gauge wires
Nile green stemtex
selection of dusting powders (petal
dusts/blossom tints)
lemon-coloured sugartex
cattleya orchid throat cutters in 2 sizes
28-gauge white wires
ceramic silk veining tool
Dresden tool
celpad
dogbone tool
Nile green floristry tape
grooved board
24-gauge green wires
peony leaf veiner
half-strength glaze

Wind cotton thread around 2 fingers and a celstick approximately 60 times. Twist into a figure-of-eight and thread a 30-gauge white wire through the centre and secure. Cut the top edge of the cotton and immerse in egg white; separate the cotton with a scriber and allow to dry.

Roll a small piece of dark brown flower paste onto an 18-gauge wire, elongating this down the stem. Roll out small pieces of flower paste into teardrop shapes and fasten to the main stem with egg white. Allow to dry. Follow the instructions in Step 1 opposite.

Roll out a piece of pale pink flower paste, leaving a ridge at the bottom. Follow the instructions in Step 2 opposite.

Place the petal on a celpad and soften the edge with a dogbone tool. Cup the centres of the petals. Allow to dry over a piece of foam sponge to keep in shape. Dust the base of the petals and the outer edge with plum dusting powder.

Make 10 smaller petals and 15 larger ones for each flower. Starting with the smaller petals, wire together to a neat and well-balanced flower. Add 2 extra 18-gauge wires to give strength and tape down with Nile green floristry tape.

To make a bud, roll a large ball of white flower paste into a cone and secure onto a hooked 18-gauge wire. Allow to dry. Follow the instructions in Step 3 opposite.

Roll out another piece of paste and cut out 3 petals with the larger cutter. Treat as for the previous layer. Secure around the cone, opening the petals more than the first 3. Allow to dry. Tape the stem with Nile green stemtex.

Using equal quantities of Christmas green, gooseberry green and spruce green paste food colourings, colour the flower paste for the leaves. Roll out over a grooved board, inserting a 24-gauge green wire as described on page 10. Cut out the leaves in various sizes, using the

~ 1 ~

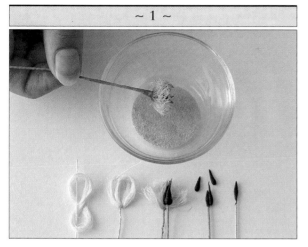

Using Nile green stemtex, secure stamens around main stem. Dust base of stem and stamens with a mixture of aubergine and plum dusting powders. Moisten tips of stamens and dip into lemon-coloured sugartex. Allow to dry.

~ 2 ~

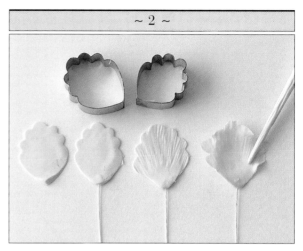

Using the larger cattleya orchid throat cutter, cut out a petal with pointed end of cutter over the ridge. Insert a hooked 28-gauge white wire into thickened paste. Vein petal using a ceramic silk veining tool. Flute edge of petal with a Dresden tool.

~ 3 ~

Roll out a piece of white flower paste and using smaller cutter, cut out 3 petals veining, softening and cupping as before. Moisten pointed ends of petals, arrange in a fan shape and fasten tightly around the cone.

~ 4 ~

LEAVES Vein with a peony leaf veiner and soften edges on a celpad, using a dogbone tool. Dust with moss green dusting powder. Darken base of leaf with plum dusting powder. Glaze with half-strength glaze.

templates below. Follow the instructions in Step 4 on page 63.

Wire the leaves together, using an 18-gauge wire for strength as shown in the photograph on page 63. Tape down the stem with Nile green floristry tape and dust the stems with plum dusting powder.

Wire the flowers and leaves together to form a well-balanced spray. This arrangement is ideal for a table decoration.

Peony leaves

Cattleya orchid cutters used to make peony petals

DUTCH IRIS

white flower paste
grooved board
white 24-gauge wire
iris petal cutters or templates, see page 68
iris veiners
Dresden tool
dogbone tool
Dried sweetcorn leaf
18-gauge wire
Nile green stemtex

To make a single iris you will have to cut out and shape 3 of each of the different petals.

Roll out a piece of white flower paste over a grooved board, laying a 24-gauge wire on top of the paste as shown on page 10. Place the iris cutter or template on top of the flower paste and cut out the shape of the broad petal. Follow the instructions in Step 1 opposite. Then replace the petal in the veiner to regain the shape.

Roll out a piece of flower paste and cut out the forked petal, using the template or iris cutter. Follow the instructions in Step 2 opposite.

Remove the frilled petal from the veiner and stick to the first petal as in Step 3. Place on a piece of foam sponge and allow to dry in shape.

Roll out another piece of flower paste over the board, laying the wire over the paste as shown on page 10. Cut out the shape, using the cutter or the template of the narrow petal. Follow the instructions in Step 4 opposite.

Replace the petal in the veiner and allow it to regain its shape. Remove from the veiner and place on a piece of foam. Allow to dry.

Next dust the petals as described in Step 3 on

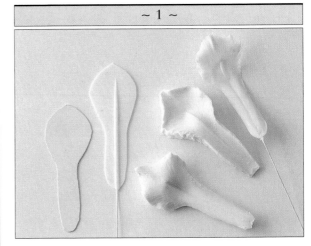

~ 1 ~

Place broad petal in veiner and vein it. Remove the petal from veiner and place on grooved board. Use a Dresden tool to flute edge of petals. Place petal on a celpad and soften edges with a dogbone tool.

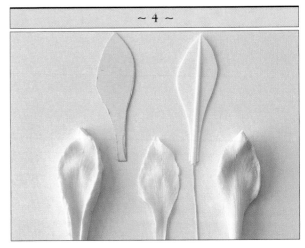

~ 4 ~

Place narrow petal in appropriate veiner and vein. Remove from veiner. Place petal on board and flute edge with a Dresden tool. Place on a celpad and soften edges with dogbone tool.

~ 2 ~

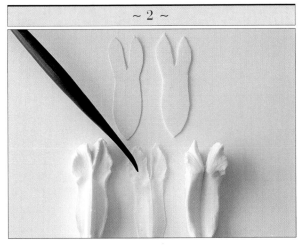

Using appropriate reiner, vein forked petal. Remove from veiner. Flute edges using Dresden tool. Replace in veiner to regain shape.

~ 3 ~

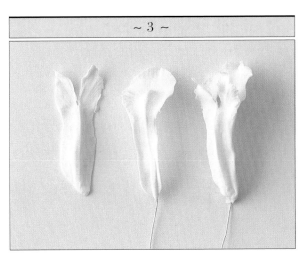

Dust inner throat of iris with lemon dusting powder, then turn petals over and dust back of wide petal with lemon and a little moss green dusting powder.

~ 5 ~

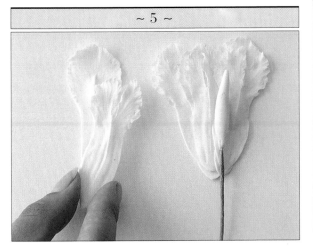

Arrange 3 petals in a fan shape, moistening base and sticking them together. Place stem with elongated piece of paste on top and wrap petals around, making sure piece of paste in centre is not visible.

~ 6 ~

Start by wiring 3 narrow petals onto wire and then adding 3 outer petals, making sure they are right way around. It is advisable to add another 18-gauge wire to form a thicker stem.

Dust the buds first on the outer centre vein of the wider petal with lemon and moss green dusting powder and then dust the rest of the petals first with lavender and then deep purple.

To wire up the iris, first cover an 18-gauge wire with Nile green stemtex, then follow the instructions in Step 6 on page 67.

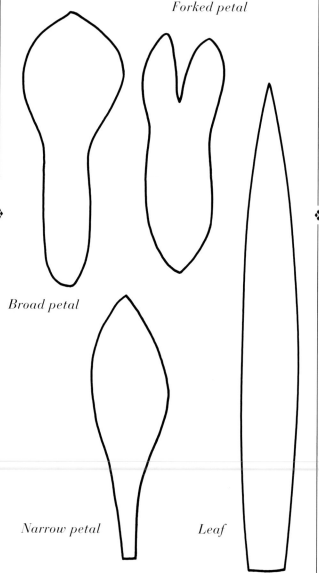

Forked petal

Broad petal

Narrow petal

Leaf

page 67. Dust the rest of the petals first with lavender dusting powder and then go over them with deep purple.

To make the leaves, roll out a piece of pale green flower paste. Cut it into a 'V' shape and vein using a piece of dried sweetcorn leaf. Place on a celpad and vein down the centre with a veining tool. Soften the edges with a dogbone tool. Moisten the centre of the leaves and wrap them around the stems of the iris.

To make the iris bud, roll a piece of white flower paste onto an 18-gauge wire, elongating it down the stem. Roll out a piece of white flower paste and cut out 3 of both the wider petal and the forked petal. Vein and flute as described above. Moisten the narrower part of the wider petals and place the forked petals on top. Follow the instructions in Step 5 on page 67.

Sundial Wedding Cake, page 12
Dial

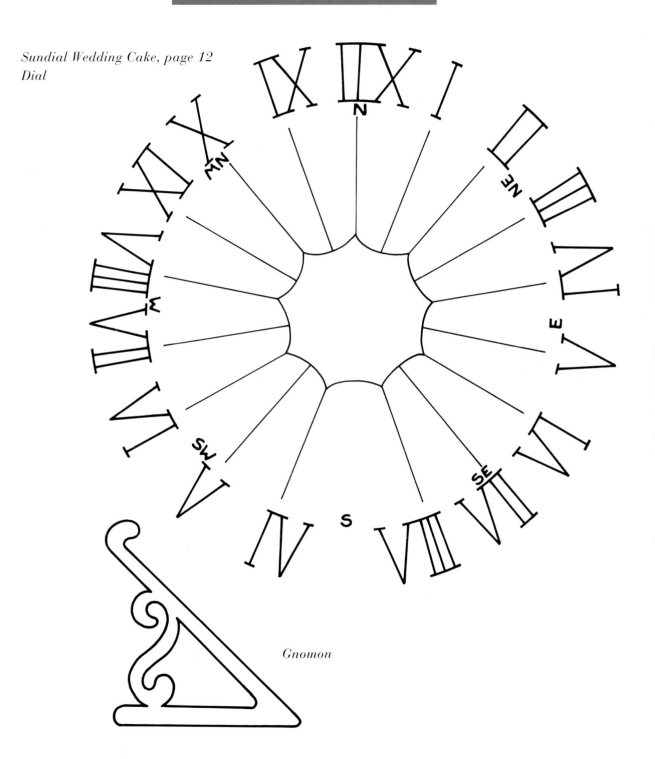

Gnomon

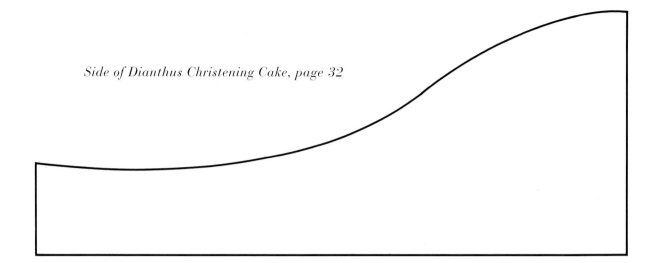

Side of Dianthus Christening Cake, page 32

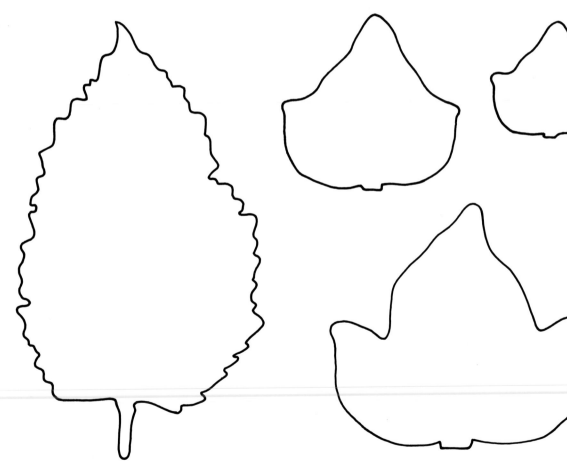

Golden Wedding Cake, page 46
Sunflower leaf

Casablanca Fantasy Wedding Cake, page 37
Ivy leaves

Casablanca Fantasy Wedding Cake, page 37

Showing position of pillars

INDEX

FOR FURTHER INFORMATION

Merehurst is the leading publisher of cake decorating books and has an excellent range of titles to suit cake decorators of all levels. Please send for a free catalogue, stating the title of this book:

United Kingdom	**U.S.A./Canada**	**Australia**	**Other Territories**
Marketing Department	*Foxwood International Ltd.*	*J.B. Fairfax Ltd.*	*For further information*
Merehurst Ltd.	*Suite 426*	*80 McLachlan Avenue*	*contact:*
Ferry House	*420 Main Street East, Unit C*	*Rushcutters Bay*	*International Sales*
51–57 Lacy Road	*Milton, Ontario*	*NSW 2011*	*Department at United*
London SW15 1PR	*L9T 5G3 Canada*	*Tel: (61) 2 361 6366*	*Kingdom address.*
Tel: 0181 780 1177	*Tel: 00 1 905 854 1305*	*Fax: (61) 2 360 6262*	
Fax: 0181 780 1714	*Fax: 00 1 905 854 0978*		